The Volunteer Choir

The Volunteer Choir

Frank Brownstead
&
Pat McCollam

The Pastoral Press • Washington, DC

ISBN: O-912405-37-6

The Pastoral Press
225 Sheridan Street, NW
Washington, D.C. 20011
(202) 723-1254

The Pastoral Press is the publications division of the National
Association of Pastoral Musicians, a membership organization
of musicians and clergy dedicated to fostering the art of musical
liturgy.

Printed in the United States of America

Contents

Introduction

Directing a church choir is indeed a labor of love. A choir director, to accomplish this task successfully, must love people, not only the people who gather for worship, but also those men and women, the members of the choir, who contribute so much of their time and talent so that the whole congregation or assembly might truly be able to experience God through prayer in its highest form, namely, sung prayer.

People who make up a choir are most often a very dedicated group of people. They love to sing. They love other people. They love God. Even though they might have little musical background or vocal training, they are willing to give of themselves so that the community might be able to express itself and to experience God through song. Many are the joys of the choir director privileged to work with such a group.

And yet, since our life in this world is not perfect, the choir director often encounters numerous problems. At times the choir members, coming as they do from various backgrounds, may not have the same liturgical and artistic vision as that of their director. They need motivation. Choir directors also must deal with such questions as absenteeism, lack of musicianship, imbalance of resources (ten sopranos and four basses), and the like.

In this booklet we share some suggestions to assist the choir director in solving many of the problems associated with the volunteer choir. These suggestions are the result of our practical experience. We hope that choir directors will find these recommendations helpful in their own work. We also hope that this book will offer them encouragement as they continue in their labor of love.

1

The Role of the Choir

Many of us remember the Sunday High Mass. The priest stood at the altar with his back to the people; the language was Latin; the people followed along with hand missals and listened to the music; the choir was in the loft singing the ordinary parts and the proper chants of the Mass. There can be little doubt that many Catholics found a source of inspiration in this type of celebration with its ritual beauty, dignity, and solemnity.

Certainly much has changed within recent decades. Nonetheless, there are numerous similarities between choirs today and those before the Second Vatican Council. Choir members are still expected to be dedicated and skillful persons who use their talents in serving the Lord and the community. Week after week they must still strive to use the most beautiful music available and sing to the best of their abilities. They still need to nurture their own spiritual lives so that they are truly worthy of their call to minister through song.

And yet the choir's role today is quite different from that of the choir singing at the High Mass some twenty-five years ago. The reason is found in one of the most significant documents issued by the Second Vatican Council, namely, the Constitution on the Sacred Liturgy. This document was not a revolutionary statement, not an attempt to impose something new and innovative upon us. On the contrary, the principles contained in the Constitution directly descend from the earliest centuries of the church's existence. They are the same standards which influenced the models of worship experienced by the early Christians. These norms attempt to bring us closer to

1

our roots, to make our worship reflect the true meaning of "liturgy" as being the "work of the people."

Just as the role of the priest has changed from celebrating Mass "for" the people to celebrating Mass "with" the people, so the choir's role has likewise changed. No longer is the choir to sing "for" the assembly. It is to sing "with" and "for" those who have gathered to worship.

Understandably, this change in the model of our worship caused a degree of confusion and anxiety among musicians who lead and train choirs. Many thought that when the pre-Vatican II "traditional" role of the choir was changed, the choir was no longer needed. Believing that the only thing left for the choir to do was to sing hymns in unison with the congregation, they felt that this was not a valid function for a choral group. They were partly correct. Unison hymn singing alone is not a valid function for a choral group. Unfortunately the fear produced by such thinking prevented numerous choir directors from exploring the many avenues open to a choir in today's liturgy.

A complaint frequently heard among some Catholics is that the change from the Latin Mass has resulted in the loss of awe, mystery, and sense of reverence once experienced in the ritual. In many cases this is true. However, the reason is not that these qualities are lacking in the revised rites, but rather that we are still learning how to express them well. We are still in the process of discovering the many ways music can be effectively used in our worship.

Nothing equals a well-prepared choir in adding beauty and solemnity to a liturgical celebration. The choir can set the tone and carry it through, be it one of joy, reverence, or penitence. The choir can bring out the hidden meaning, highlight the important word, help us reach out to others, help us get in touch with ourselves. The bishops of the United States in their document *Music in Catholic Worship* clearly emphasize this point.

A well-trained choir adds beauty and solemnity to the liturgy and also assists and encourages the singing of the congregation. The Second Vatican Council, speaking of the choir, stated emphatically: "Choirs must be diligently promoted," provided that "the whole body of the faithful may be able to contribute that active participation which is rightfully theirs."

"At times the choir, within the congregation of the faithful and as part of it, will assume the role of leadership, while at other times it will retain its own distinctive ministry. This means that the choir will lead the people in sung prayer, by alternating or reinforcing the sacred song of the congregation, or by enhancing it with the addition of musical elaboration. At other times in the course of liturgical celebration the choir alone will sing works whose musical demands enlist and challenge its competence." (*Music in Catholic Worship*, Revised Edition, 1983, Article 36)

From this we see that the role of the choir today is twofold— that of leadership and that of enhancement. This is a dynamic role, one that is both challenging and exciting. Although we are certainly bound by the rules of good liturgy, good music, and common sense, there is abundant room for creativity in liturgy today.

The choir that sincerely strives to fulfill this role mandated by the Second Vatican Council will seek out beautiful settings of service music and hymns that foster and enhance participation, making it exciting for the assembly, and yet at the same time allowing for creativity and challenge on the part of the choir. Such a choir will choose anthems and motets that correspond to the liturgy of the day. Through the offering of its musical gifts the choir will deepen insight and add fuller meaning to word and sacrament. When this is the case, there will be no question of whether the choir is needed or has a vital role in the liturgical celebration. Its members will be seen as a blessing to the community.

The role of the cantor as its relates to the choir is relevant here. Some believe that when the choir is present it takes over the leadership role of the cantor, who then becomes superfluous. This couldn't be farther from the truth. The cantor has two primary roles, namely, to sing the verses of the psalms, and to lead the singing of the assembly. Even when a choir is present, these functions are best done by a single person. If the choir is singing a hymn or piece of service music of any complexity and expects the full assembly to participate, a cantor is essential to assure that the congregation feels secure in its part. Also, a good working relationship between the cantor and choir is an eloquent sign of unity in the assembly.

At times the placement of the choir poses a question. Ideally, the choir, as part of the assembly, should be in close proximity to the people. If the choir is located toward the front of the church, special care must be taken to assure perfect deportment.

Another frequent question concerns the choir members wearing or not wearing special clothing. Choir robes tend to invest the choir with a certain dignity and add an ambience of festivity and solemnity to the celebration. They also insure uniform and appropriate dress for choir members. However, there are those who feel that even though the choir is a particular group, to set them apart in this way detracts from their role as members of the assembly.

However these and other questions are resolved, the important thing to remember is that it is the duty and joy of the choir, as the servant of the assembly, to raise heart and voice in praise of God.

Possibilities for Choir Participation

Flexibility is extremely important for the choir's participation in the the liturgy. The choir must not fall into a rut in terms of which parts it sings or the manner in which they are sung. Here are a few possibilities.

1. *Before Mass.* The choir can sing an anthem or motet to set the mood or atmosphere of the celebration.

2. *Entrance.* A hymn involving both people and choir may be used. For example, the choir may sing in harmony or add descants while the assembly sings in unison. Or, the assembly and the choir may alternate verses. On some occasions a choir selection (for example, the Introit sung from the Roman Gradual) may be sung.

3. *Penitential Rite.* This is often recited, especially if the Glory to God is sung. And yet simple responses to the litany may be sung by congregation and choir. During Advent and Lent (particularly Lent) it might be appropriate for the choir to sing the Kyrie eleison. But, for heaven sakes, don't sing the Kyrie and then recite the Glory to God.

4. *Glory to God.* This is a hymn and since hymns are ineffective when spoken, choose from one of the many ways of singing the text: choir and people throughout; people singing a refrain with the choir singing the verses; choir alone. From time to time it might be permissible to sing the text in Latin.

5. *Alleluia.* The whole assembly is to sing this acclamation, and yet the options for choir enhancement are many.

6. *Creed.* The Profession of Faith is best recited.

7. *Preparation of the Gifts.* The choir may sing anthems or motets, but a hymn or instrumental music may be used as well.

8. *Acclamations during the Eucharistic Prayer.* These include the

Holy, Holy, the Memorial Acclamation, and the Great Amen. The assembly is always to participate, and yet the options for choral embellishment are numerous.

9. *Lord's Prayer.* The Our Father may be sung or recited, depending on what achieves the best liturgical balance in a given situation.

10. *Lamb of God.* This litany, like the Kyrie, is an opportunity for flexibility.

11. *Distribution of the Eucharist.* The singing of hymns or of psalmody (responsorial or antiphonal) by the whole assembly symbolizes the unity of the faithful as they share the body and blood of Christ. However, for this to work well, the music must be like a reflex. It must be very familiar. While the people sing in unison, the choir can add beauty through descants and harmony. At times the choir alone may sing during the eucharistic distribution or afterwards, as an aid to the prayer of the assembly.

12. *Recessional.* While the ministers depart, the choir alone may sing, or the people may sing a hymn which the choir adorns with harmony and descants.

One of the most important factors here is to be attentive to the balance between word and song, the balance between assembly and choir. When this balance is attained, when the nature of the season and the particular character of the Mass as determined by the readings are respected, then the liturgy will be rich in solemnity and beauty.

2

Developing a Sense of Ministry

Recent years have witnessed a rapid development of lay ministries in the Catholic Church. Many communities have ministers to the elderly, the sick, the divorced, the widowed. There are eucharistic ministers, youth ministers, and music ministers. Indeed, the term "ministry" is so tossed around that it has become something of a buzzword. We can be tempted to assume the title "minister" without necessarily adopting the attitudes integral to ministry. This is perfectly understandable when we consider the dichotomy which exists in the ministerial role. To minister means to serve the community—to place oneself at the disposal of others. However, in most instances, the minister is also the one who leads—the one who has responsibility and makes the important decisions, the one who has the most knowledge and expertise in a particular area. When a person continually functions as a leader, it is all too easy to forget the servant aspect of one's role.

As music ministers we must continually balance our desire to make beautiful music with the needs of the community and with the requirements of the liturgy. Is our music truly intended as a service to the assembly? Or is the reason for what we do to be found elsewhere? Do we actually view ourselves as first of all members of the assembly, yet members with a special gift to offer? Or do we feel that we are set apart, somehow above everyone else? We must always keep in mind that our talents were given to us for the good of the community. Far from making us feel set apart or superior, this knowledge should fill us with humility and make us constantly aware of our responsibility to place our gifts at the service of all.

Part of our responsibility as leaders and directors of choirs is to see to it that choir members understand their unique role in the ministry of music. Long past are the days when the choir saw itself as an elite group performing all the music at Mass. Certainly the post-Vatican II vision encourages and even mandates choirs to perform beautiful music as a stimulus to the assembly's prayer. And yet, and more importantly, today's choir must also support, encourage, and nurture the active participation of all.

Fostering a ministerial attitude in your choir begins with you, the choir director, and the way you deal with the choir members. For instance, it is important that you know each member by name, that you evidence care and concern for them individually, especially when they have special needs, problems, hardships, or sorrows. Little things mean a lot, and a card, phone call, or a kind word from you will be appreciated and remembered. Also, encourage choir members to be caring toward one another. Begin by helping them get to know one another through breaks at rehearsals and at social gatherings throughout the year. Be sure to include prayer as part of each rehearsal. Whether brief or lengthy, prayer should be included in every rehearsal. During this time be sure to mention by name those choir members who are sick. Invite all present to voice their individual concerns. Lead the choir in prayer for the spirit of ministry. "O God our Father, thank you for the gift of music. May we serve you and others through the talents you have given us." Help the choir members understand service not only as a privilege but also as a duty inherent in baptism.

In other words, form the choir into a warm, caring group of people who love, welcome, and serve one another first. This has all sorts of wonderful side effects. Choir members begin to feel they are part of an extended family. Such an attitude encourages accountability to the group, a cordial attitude toward newcomers, and better and better singing.

It is essential that you instill into the choir a sense of care and concern for the whole assembly. For example, explain to the members why they can't as yet sing the descant to a new hymn—the assembly doesn't know the hymn well enough and still needs support on the melody. On special occasions have the choir take part in the entrance procession, even if it means walking down the center aisle, up the sides, and back into the choir loft. Explain that this carries their beautiful full-voiced singing of the entrance hymn throughout the church and offers a wonderful example to the community of how hymn singing should sound. Make it a priority that the choir thoroughly knows any new congregational music, even a unison hymn, before the Sunday morning the piece is to be introduced. In this way the choir can effectively support the assembly. If the choir is learning new music at the same time as the people, then the choir's members will not feel that are exercising a leadership role. Frequently point out what a difference it makes to the singing of a unison hymn when the choir is participating with full-voiced enthusiasm.

Use settings of service music, psalms, and hymns that have a refrain for the congregation and more elaborate parts for the choir, for example, settings of the Gloria by John Foley, Richard Proulx, Alex Peloquin; the Sanctus from "A Festival Eucharist" by Proulx; "We Rely on the Power of God" by Richard Hillert. There are some marvelous compositions in this style. (See the repertory listing at the end of this book.) Such music adds much festivity to the celebration and allows for participation without overtaxing the assembly.

Remember that if you approach this aspect of choir work positively, as an exciting way of nurturing the congregation's song, then the choir will take pride in the way the people participate and respond. If, however, you see working with the assembly as a boring chore forced upon you, then the choir will also adopt this attitude. After all, isn't the assembly the principal choir?

A further aspect of ministerial attitude is openness toward other musicians in the parish. For instance, have you ever tried to combine forces with the folk group (or traditional choir) on special occasions? Have you ever tried teaching your group one of "their" pieces or suggesting that "they" learn one of yours, so that the two choirs might sing something together? This can work, at least in a limited way, and is a wonderful sign of the oneness of the ministry of music. Fortunately, we have many compositions available to us that are suitable for various types of ensembles. Again, the success or failure of this approach will depend a great deal on your personal attitude.

Finally, there is the assembly's responsibility to minister to the ministers—in this case, to affirm the choir and to show appreciation for its work. This usually needs to be initiated by the leader of the assembly—the pastor, or the priest who presides at the Mass. Most clergy are happy to acknowledge the choir from time to time. They just don't think of it on their own. Why not remind them? "Father, the choir was here for the Holy Thursday liturgy, for Good Friday, Holy Saturday, and now again this morning, Easter Sunday. Would you please extend a word of thanks to them toward the end of Mass?" Another approach is to suggest a simple blessing ritual for the choir on the last Sunday the choir sings before the summer recess. Most pastors are happy to do this, especially if the choir director prepares the text. One format is for the presider to make a few comments on the work the choir does throughout the year and how this benefits the community. He then asks the choir to stand for a special blessing. (A beautiful and appropriate text can be prepared by using as a model the blessing formulas found in the sacramentary.) The assembly then acknowledges its appreciation through applause. Such public acknowledgement makes the choir feel appreciated and also raises the assembly's consciousness about the contribution made by the choir. This is not fishing for compliments. Rather, it is a means whereby the choir director can minister to the choir members so that they in turn might be motivated to minister even more effectively. If you have a pastor who takes the initiative in this regard, you are fortunate indeed. And yet the ministry of music is just one of the many areas of concern to the clergy of the parish. They genuinely appreciate suggestions and ideas, especially if offered in a kind, helpful, and uncritical fashion.

Above all, foster your own spirit of ministry. Allow the Spirit to work within you. If you are a good leader, the choir members will respect you and spontaneously look to you for guidance. One good example is worth a thousand words. The choir will respond far better if what you say is firmly rooted in what you do.

3

The Choir Outside Ritual

Although a parish choir exists to sing during the community's liturgical celebrations, this need not be the only opportunity for the choir to sing. In fact, performances in non-liturgical settings have numerous benefits, many of which may well improve the choir's musicianship when it sings at worship.

The preparation and performance of a concert or special program can be most beneficial for a choir. The purpose of a concert is to communicate through the idiom of music, to present music for its own sake. When the goal is communication through music, singers are motivated to work hard to improve the quality of their singing. Such a musical outlet is both challenging and stimulating. The novice choir, when presenting a special program, could employ music that though simple is nevertheless of high quality. Perhaps the music could be just slightly more difficult than the music ordinarily sung during the liturgy. For the sake of variety the special event might include a few instruments, special soloists, the participation of small groups (duets, trios, quartets, and the like). An advantage here is that this relieves the choir of the burden of preparing a lengthy program. Since the skills of the choir will improve through this process, special projects of this kind have an impact on the music sung during the liturgy. Certainly the morale and confidence of the choir will improve. And the best result of all? The concert is likely to be a wonderful recruitment tool.

Since a small choir might lack the resources necessary for

presenting a special program or concert, it is often advantageous to combine two or three choirs for an event to be presented in several locations. Consider combining the parish choir with other church choirs, synagogue choirs, community choirs, school or university choral groups. Directors might want to share conducting duties at each concert, or conduct the entire concert at one's own location, or follow some variation of these options. Calculate rehearsal time so that the singers have ample opportunity to acquaint themselves with a new conductor, with an orchestra, or with a different physical setting.

More proficient choirs might want to tackle larger, more challenging works. Singing with an orchestra is always a special thrill, and many of the larger works (cantatas and oratorios) present fascinating opportunities for growth on the part of both singers and audience.

Another idea is to combine entertainment, music, and good food by having the choir present a dinner theater. This might offer an opportunity for participation by singers from the parish who are not regular choir members. It is also a wonderful social occasion. Along the same lines is the Madrigal Dinner. Confer Paul Brandvik's *The Compleet Madrigal Booke* (Knight-shtick Press, Box 814, Depart. A, Bemidji MN 56601). This can be as simple or as complicated as one wishes. Such experiences have been very popular in many parishes and they offer a good outlet for the choir.

Also consider involving the choir in outside activities that will help develop choral skills. A choir that is improving includes individual singers who are improving. Nothing encourages growth more than the motivation of a contest, workshop, convention, or outside performance.

Another possibility is to share beautiful singing with those outside the parish community, for example, by caroling in the neighborhood, singing at a rest home or hospital, or even touring Europe on a grand scale. It might mean a fund raising concert for some worthy cause or a visit to a church in a nearby city.

If a choir wants to grow in every way, then its individual members must certainly grow spiritually. How about a choir retreat? Perhaps one with all the ministers of the parish present. Furthermore, purely social events are always useful in fostering camaraderie among the members of the choir.

4

Recruiting

Let's face it, developing a church choir to a reasonable and practical size is a difficult task. For the most part, people are not camped on our doorsteps begging to join parish choirs. Not only does membership in a choir requires a formidable commitment of time, but only a limited group of people qualify. Also, choir membership usually precludes the family participating together at Mass. It ties one to a Sunday schedule that often interferes with family activities. Furthermore, the choir can appear to be an exclusive group, a group inhibiting would-be recruits. Although "numbers for numbers' sake" is certainly not a worthwhile goal, the choir should be able to produce a full sound in a particular environment. The group should have enough people so that an emergency does not exist if three or four members are absent on a Sunday morning.

Even if the choir is already large, you should give time and thought to recruiting new singers since choir membership seldom stays the same for long. People move away, become sick (or have loved ones who become ill), experience a birth in the family, or become interested in other endeavors. You may occasionally have to ask someone to leave because of sporadic attendance or an unacceptable attitude. Besides, recruiting is a way of giving people who might not otherwise come forward an opportunity to join. It evidences an open and inviting attitude which should be the hallmark of any group committed to ministry. This does not mean that you should allow the "tone deaf" and the "gravel voiced" to join forces with you. Rather, it means that you should seek out and welcome those who have a legitimate place in this ministry.

Unless you are just beginning a choir, recruiting will usually yield anywhere from one to twelve new people at any one time, depending on how you proceed. A bulletin or pulpit announcement may gain one or two new recruits. A personal invitation to specific people, having choir members greet people after Mass each Sunday, these will also bring in a few people over a period of time. If the choir recesses for the summer, you might try a summer choir in which you invite anyone to come and sing, even families with children, with the only rehearsal taking place the hour before Mass. Often people will so enjoy this experience that they will try out for the regular choir in the fall. Some directors are very creative about recruiting. One composed a little recruiting song which was sung by the choir at the announcement time on recruiting Sunday.

(*in pseudo-choral style*)

We invite you to join us
For our special open rehearsal,
We meet to glorify God,
Practice great music,
And have funnnnnnnn!
Whether you are soprano, alto, tenor, or bass,
Please consider yourself welcome
At 7:30 Thursday in the loft.

Chorus

Check it out, check it out, check it out!

(Honora Kelley, used with permission.)

Another director, whose choir doesn't sing every week, sits in the midst of the assembly on the "off" Sundays and tries to pick out people with really good voices and speaks to them after the

Mass. The secret of successful recruiting is to do it consistently, regularly, year after year, preferably at specific times, for example, every September, or every September and January. Do not expect membership to increase dramatically in one effort, but aim for steady growth over a period of several years. Membership will be much more solid.

One method which has proved very successful consists of the following seven steps which can be followed once or twice a year.

Step One. Designate a specific Sunday as choir recruiting Sunday. This should be coordinated with the parish calendar so that, ideally, it doesn't fall on Religious Education Sunday, Boy/Girl Scout Sunday, or any Sunday when something extra is already taking place. On the Sunday preceding your recruiting day place an announcement in the bulletin about the choir—when you rehearse and sing, who can join, what the advantages of membership are. Include a name and phone number. Add that recruiting will take place the following Sunday.

Senior Choir: *Do you have a good voice? Musical talent? Choir experience? Now is a good time to join the Senior Choir and share your gifts with our parish community. We rehearse on Thursday evening from 8:00 to 10:00 p.m. and sing each Sunday morning at the 9:30 a.m. Mass. We also sing for other liturgies and frequently have an opportunity to participate in diocesan and inter-diocesan events. We will have a sign-up table on the patio next weekend. For further information call . . .*

Step Two. On recruiting Sunday have an announcement regarding the choir read at each liturgy. The message should include such information as the day and time of rehearsals, time of the Sunday Mass at which the choir sings, who may join, as well as any interesting facts about the choir, for example, special concerts, special music being planned, and the like. The announcement should be as brief as possible, no longer than a minute and a half, and should be well-prepared, well-delivered, and enjoyable for the people to hear. Since the director or the members have more enthusiasm for the choir than anyone else, it is best to have them make the announcement. If choir members will be performing this task, you will probably need a different person for each Mass. But don't ask for volunteers. Rather, choose men and women who can deliver the message effectively and present a good public appearance. Projecting a good image is extremely important since first impressions greatly influence people. You may want to let your speakers prepare their own messages, but give them some written guidelines as to the maximum length of the announcement and the information to be included. If you choose to make the announcement yourself, the same principles about public speaking and appearance also apply to you.

If your parish has a policy that only the priest or another specified minister may make announcements, write out what you want them to say. Be sure that the text is well-written and neatly typed. Having an extra copy handy will prove beneficial in case the original is lost or misplaced between Masses.

Step Three. Have a sign-up table (tables) outside the church where interested people can leave their names and phone numbers. It is useful if one or more choir members are at each table so that they might answer questions. Make sure the table is clearly labeled as the choir sign-up location. It is also helpful to run your bulletin announcement from the preceding Sunday on this Sunday also. That way, if prospective members don't stop by your table, they may call later on.

Step Four. On Sunday evening or the next day at the latest phone everyone who has signed up. Initial enthusiasm tends to wane quickly if immediate action is not taken. Inquire as to what previous experience, if any, the prospective members have, whether they can read music, and what voice part they sing or think they sing. Reiterate the day and time of rehearsals and the time the choir sings on Sunday. This will avoid future misunderstandings. Unless you have an exceptionally good memory, take notes as you are talking. Write down pertinent facts and any information that will help you in subsequent meetings to welcome these new people and make them feel at ease. Also, during the phone interview make an appointment to audition each recruit. These auditions can be done very quickly—you can usually schedule them at ten minute intervals and complete the whole process in under two hours. However, be extremely cautious about using the word "audition" unless you are dealing with seasoned singers. It is far less scary just to ask the recruits to come and sing for you, explaining that you need to get an idea of their range, volume, and timbre. Also, during the phone call, inform the prospective members of the date and time of an orientation rehearsal that you have scheduled, and also of the date of the first regular rehearsal you expect them to attend. Explain that the orientation rehearsal is a special time for them to get together with you before they attend a regular rehearsal. Its purpose is to acquaint the new people with the routine procedures the choir follows and to familiarize them with some of the music the choir regularly sings, for example, Mass settings.

Step Five. At the audition it is important to take time to put the new people at ease. Smile when you greet each one for the first time. Be sure you know their names. Take a minute to chat before you begin the audition. Be positive and encouraging as you go through the process.

The degree of difficulty required in the audition will be related to the degree of skill required of new members. If the choir is open to anyone who has a pleasant voice and can "carry a tune," then the process is fairly simple. For instance, you can take a five note descending scale and, using the syllable "ya," have the auditioning singer begin in a median range. Continue the exercise up by half steps till you reach the top of the range. Then go back to the original starting note and move down by half steps till the bottom range is reached. By this time you will have a fairly good idea of whether the singer can match pitch, and you will certainly know if any vocal problems are present. Next, using a syllable such as "ya," "mi," "loo," and the like, you can play or sing musical patterns and ask the singer to sing these back to you. These exercises can be made increasingly difficult, for example, do,re,mi,re,do; do,mi,sol,mi,do; do,re, mi,fa,sol,mi,do. Gordon Lamb's *Choral Exercises* is a good resource for such patterns. This procedure will tell you how well the recruit can match pitch and also give you an idea of how much the person can retain. If you require music reading skills, you will also want to include some time for sight singing in the audition.

One of the most difficult tasks of a choir director is telling people that they don't measure up to the standards required for joining the choir. True, some problems can be corrected in rehearsals, but beware of persons who cannot match pitch or have major vocal problems. It is far better to tell them gently and kindly on the spot that they need to correct the difficulty through voice lessons or enrollment in a basic music theory class before being eligible for choir membership than to bear the burden of an unsuitable voice for years to come. In this type of situation it may be appropriate to direct the person to a different ministry. Many have gifts that qualify them as eucharistic ministers, readers, teachers of religion, and the like. If you point out that the community needs people with such gifts, they are often quite happy to serve in other areas of parish ministry.

After the audition has been successfully completed, distribute written material about choir membership. It is good to have a paper to hand out that includes information about specific choir policies, for example, attendance rules or guidelines, procedures for acquiring robes and music, and so forth. The booklet *What Every Choir Member Should Know* by H. Myron Braun (Pastoral Arts Associates) is also useful, especially for those who have not previously been members of a choir.

You may wish to develop an information form for new members. It should include all pertinent information—name, address, phone number, birthday (if you want to acknowledge birthdays), vocal part, and any other information that will be useful to you (Do you play a musical instrument? Do you need transportation?).

Step Six. The purpose of the orientation rehearsal is to make it easier for recruits to become comfortable with choir format and procedure. Often, especially for those who have very little or no previous choir background, the integration process is so overwhelming that they become discouraged and leave before they have an opportunity to "settle in." Even for more experienced recruits, starting cold into an already existing group can be quite intimidating.

Have one or two members from each section of the choir help out at the orientation rehearsal. Ideally these members should be both good singers and hospitable people. Introduce everyone. Spend some time explaining procedures. Do you list the order of music for rehearsal and how does a person find the music listed? Is it in alphabetical order, by number, by composer, or by title? Do you use a standard format for communicating what will be sung at Mass and when? When do the choir members receive the eucharist? What about robes? Do members have their own music? Is it assigned by number? Can they take it home?

It also helps to explain that it will take some time for the new members to become familiar with the music the choir already knows. Also mention that there will be music that everyone in the choir is just beginning to learn.

Go over the music that you use regularly, and include some of the pieces that will be practiced in the first regular rehearsal the recruits will attend. Be candid about not having time to go over the music thoroughly at this particular time. Mention that there will be lots of support in the regular rehearsal.

Step Seven. Before the regular rehearsal make sure that the choir knows that new members are coming for the first time. Encourage old-timers to be friendly and welcoming. Have everyone wear nametags, and be sure copies of all music are ready for the new people. Decide in advance where you want them to sit. Direct them there as they come in. At the beginning of the rehearsal introduce the new people, and perhaps have the regular members introduce themselves and tell how long they've been in the choir. It's a great icebreaker. Don't attempt to tailor the pace of the rehearsal to the new people—by this time they shouldn't expect it. However, you can seat them beside stronger singers. At this rehearsal it is advantageous to take a fairly long break (fifteen minutes or so) and, if possible, to have simple refreshments. This makes the new members feel welcome and helps them become acquainted.

All this may sound very complicated and demanding, but it is much easier to accomplish than it is to describe. Moreover, it happens only once or twice a year. If possible, the whole integration process can and should be completed between recruiting Sunday and the time of the next regular rehearsal. Have auditions on a Monday and Tuesday, the orientation rehearsal on Tuesday or Wednesday, and then have the new members present for the regular Wednesday or Thursday choir rehearsal.

This process will usually yield six to twelve new members for the choir. A few may drop out during the first week or two, but most will remain and become faithful members of the group.

Perhaps you are faced with starting a choir from "scratch." This can be an exciting and rewarding job if you approach it with the proper attitude. You are starting a new ministry in your community and opening up new vistas, not only for those who will form the choir but also for the whole parish. You will certainly want to obtain much publicity and do regular recruiting. But even before this you may want to gather a group of people to form the nucleus of the choir. One approach might be to form a "Festival Choir" for a special parish event—a group that would meet and rehearse for several weeks previous to a single occasion. Or you might begin by developing a choir that would sing for special times of the liturgical year, for example, the Christmas season or the Easter season.

Whatever type of recruiting best suits your particular situation, it is essential to remember that the most effective recruiting device is a choir that sings well and has an exciting program. People do not want to join a group that sounds bad; they will not remain members of a group that is in a rut. This is an excellent reason to consider hiring paid section leaders. Certainly the purpose of the choir is not to show off but rather to minister to the assembly. There is nothing more powerful and beautiful than a liturgy where an excellent choir lends its voice to support the prayer of all. If you are restricted by a lack of talent in the group, one good musician in each section or problem section makes a dramatic difference. This enables you to accomplish more at each rehearsal and to work on more challenging music since it will also attract other skilled people to the group. Section leaders often can also function as cantors. The benefits far outweigh the cost.

5

Rehearsal Organization

Although choir directors have widely differing opinions on
how a choral group should sound or how a piece of music
should be approached, most will agree on at least two points:
rehearsal time is precious; there is never enough of it. Most of
us see our choirs once a week for an hour and a half, perhaps
two hours, and we always have volumes of material to cover.
Therefore, it is essential to make the most of every minute of
practice time.

The key to successful rehearsals is to plan, plan, and plan.
Without careful planning, both long and short term, and
without specific goals in mind, it is really impossible to budget
time effectively.

Begin by making a general plan of all the music the choir will
sing for the entire year. Do this during the summer months.
Review the liturgical calendar for the year and decide what
music you want to use that is already on hand and what new
music you will need to order. If buying a large amount of new
music all at once is a financial strain for the parish, draw up a
purchasing schedule for the year. Make a master rehearsal
schedule for the year. This should take into account how far in
advance you need to start each piece. For new music, a good
rule of thumb is to allow six weeks of lead time.

Plan each rehearsal carefully on a week to week basis. Have
in mind specific objectives as well as a general time frame for

each piece you rehearse, for example, five minutes to read through "Draw Us in the Spirit's Tether," and ten minutes to solve the rhythm problems in measures ten to twenty of "If Ye Love Me." The music should not be rehearsed in a random order. Find a format that works for the group, and then follow it.

For example, one way to structure a rehearsal is to practice first the most difficult music or that which is most imminent (usually what will be sung the following Sunday). Then vary the remaining pieces so that you have a combination of loud-soft, hard-easy, sixteenth-eighteenth century, rather than a number of similar pieces following one another.

Another possibility is to begin the rehearsal with something that is a guaranteed success, usually a relatively easy and well-known composition. This satisfies the human need to feel successful, sets a positive tone that carries on through the evening, and motivates the singers to work hard and be cooperative. Rehearse the hardest music one-fourth to one-third of the way into the session, with the easier pieces toward the end. Conclude, as you began, with a composition that will be successful. In this way people will leave with a good feeling and will look forward to returning the following week.

Whichever order you select, post it where it can be seen by all. Use a chalkboard. If you don't have access to one, purchase a large pad of newsprint from a stationery store. It comes in a variety of sizes, costs under ten dollars, and one pad will last all year. Teach the choir members to obtain their music and arrange it in order as soon as they arrive.

Be punctual in starting rehearsals, even if only one or two singers are present. Obviously this saves time. But more than anything else, it encourages promptness on the part of the singers. A major reason for tardiness is that people know the rehearsal won't start on time anyway. Or that it really won't accomplish much during the first fifteen or twenty minutes. If tardiness is a long-standing tradition with the group, you must be careful about what music you place at the beginning of the rehearsal till the problem is corrected. Don't practice Sunday's anthem if only one or two people are present. Ending promptly also saves time. People are much more willing to remain disciplined and focused till the end of the evening if they know that there *is* an end.

In order to start on time, the director must be present well in advance and have everything ready by the time the choir arrives. The room should be neat and clean—no litter lying around. Chairs should be arranged in order. The sequence of pieces to be rehearsed should be posted. This says much about the respect you have for the singers and the value you place on their contribution. Complete your preparations ten minutes before the rehearsal begins so that you are free to greet the choristers as they arrive. Have assigned seating. This helps situate key people for maximum effectiveness and gives the singers a sense of individuality. Furthermore, it is psychologically more difficult to be absent if you know "your seat" will be vacant.

Remember that the evening is generally a passive time. Since most people come to choir rehearsal after a full day's work, they are often tired. Consequently, if you want a dynamic rehearsal, you must energize the singers. To do this you need to be energetic. If you are tired and listless, this will be reflected in the group. It is important for you to obtain some rest before the session. Encourage the singers to talk to one another and to you as they arrive. Start the rehearsal with something physical— stretch arms up high, do deep breathing exercises, or give each other back rubs. Be cheerful and positive.

Vocalizing can be a helpful tool or a mere waste of time. If you use vocal exercises simply to warm up the voice, this objective can just as well be accomplished with one of the simpler pieces you would rehearse anyway. However, if you use exercises to work toward specific goals (for example, to teach correct breathing and support, to encourage an open throat, to address problems that will arise in special pieces during the rehearsal), then these exercises are valuable.

Study thorougly each piece of music before the choir ever sees it. Know every entrance, every key and meter change. Have a clear idea of how you want the end product to sound. This does not mean that you may not change your mind as you go along. You probably will. And yet nothing will more weaken your leadership ability in the choir's eyes than not knowing the musical score. When beginning a new piece, have the singers read all the way through the composition the first time you rehearse it. No matter how poor the singing may be, this gives at least some idea of how the finished product will sound. This procedure is an important part of the learning process. It also improves the group's ability to sight read.

Don't let the atmosphere become oppresive. If you're working on a difficult passage or selection and the choir is becoming frustrated, do something to lighten everyone's spirits. Tell a joke, recount something humorous that happened during the week, or laugh at an amusing incident that involved yourself. Learning more readily occurs in a relaxed rather than in a tense setting.

Use sectional rehearsals. An accompanist, if you have one, can rehearse part of the choir while you take the rest. But if you are an organist- director, then find someone in your group who plays the piano and let this member help with the sectional.

Establish a connection between what you say and what you expect the choir to do. In other words, once you tell the choir what you want (for example, don't breathe here, sing this passage forte), make sure they do it every time the situation recurs. This means, of course, that your ears always have to be open.

Don't spend a lot of time talking. It is much more profitable to demonstrate what you want rather than trying to explain it. The people came to sing. Let them do it. When making corrections and changes, explain one thing at a time and have the choir try it immediately. Talking about several issues all at once merely confuses the singers. Make references according to page, line, and measure numbers—and in that order. Teach the singers to do the same.

Don't be afraid to try something new. Be flexible. If your rehearsal plan is all wrong one week, discard it and do what seems to be right. Be open to changes of interpretation, provided the authentic spirit of the composition is preserved.

Taking a break during the rehearsal is important since it helps people to know one another and function better as a group. If the rehearsal is longer than an hour and a half, a break is essential since everyone (yourself included) needs a rest. The break need only be a few minutes long, and refreshments are not necessary. In fact, having refreshments can make it difficult to get everyone back to work in a reasonable amount of time. Why not take the break about two-thirds of the way through the rehearsal rather than at the halfway point? Usually enough momentum develops to get you this far without much difficulty. Furthermore, it is much easier to resume work knowing that there is less than half of the job yet to be done. If you make announcements, it is wise to do so immediately before the break. This makes the break seem longer, and you eliminate the problem of people missing important information because they have arrived late or will leave early.

Incorporate some form of prayer in the rehearsal. We make music to praise the Lord and serve his people. The group could pray either at the beginning, during, or at the conclusion of the rehearsal. Each week have a different choir member assume responsibility for the prayer. Choose a hymn that says something about the ministry of the group and use it to open or conclude the prayer. Why not utilize the coming Sunday's scriptural selections as the basis for the prayer? This time for common prayer need not be lengthy, yet it should be constant part of the rehearsal.

Organize and use a system for filing and distributing music. One method is to assign each singer a folder number. Number all the pieces of music. Have designated shelves or slots where the choir members may keep their folders. Place new music in the folders or in the place where the folders are located if the people are allowed to take the music home. Have "used" music turned in periodically—every six weeks or so. It is usually possible to obtain a volunteer from the choir to serve as music librarian so that the director doesn't have to handle these organizational details. In most cases there are people in the group who enjoy this task and feel a real sense of ownership and pride in assuming such a responsibility.

Absenteeism can plague the volunteer choir, but there are remedies for the problem. Establish a policy and carry it through. This might be in the form of a *rule,* for example, that a specific number of successive unexcused absences results in dismissal. Or the policy might be in the form of a more general *guideline,* for example, if a choir member each month regularly misses more than one rehearsal or liturgy at which the choir sings, then that person should consider taking a leave of absence. Require the singers to phone in if they will be absent. Draw up an attendance sheet and assign someone to take roll, both at rehearsals and on Sundays. Each week before rehearsal give the sheet to the person in charge of attendance and have it returned to you on Sunday after Mass. Review it before the next rehearsal and send reminder cards to those who were absent and didn't check in by phone. Make sure the choir knows you keep this record, but do so in a positive way. ("Only four people out of forty were absent last Sunday. That is very good attendance." Or - "Eight people were absent from rehearsal last Thursday. I know we can do much better than that.") The problem of absenteeism never goes away. Thus you have to stay on top of it all the time. Frequently explain your expectations to the group. Special recognition for people who are seldom or never absent is also good motivation.

If you have difficulty solving problems in the choir, especially problems relating to vocal production and choral sound, contact the music departments of local colleges and universities. Enroll in a course in choral development or choral techniques (not choral conducting). Most schools will allow you to take a single course if you have good reason, even if you're not enrolled in a formal program. It may also be useful to find a reputable director in a high school or college who has a beginning choir, not an advanced one. Request permission to sit in on rehearsals for a while, especially at the beginning of the year. Join the local chapter of the Choral Conductors Guild and attend its meetings. This organization is for all choir directors, not just "professionals," and there are many practical ideas and useful information available through this source. To obtain information about your local chapter, contact a knowledgeable conductor at one of your area's churches or colleges.

6

Rehearsal Techniques

There are many books explaining choral techniques and development. The serious conductor will surely want to read as many of these as possible. But there are a few ideas which may serve as a framework on which to fasten specific techniques.

First, keep in mind that our overall goal is communication. We are attempting to share beauty with the listeners; we are trying to get across principles that are directly connected to the spiritual growth which is the purpose of our coming together. If we remember our purpose, then our rehearsals are likely to be on the right track. The goal is worth any amount of work. If it is shared by each singer, then vocal miracles are possible.

Only when each singer has a real understanding of this goal and believes in it, can trust be developed between the director and the singers. This trust is necessary if the choir is to grow in its ministry. And once trust has been established, the director can begin to solve specific musical problems.

To attain a particular musical result, the director must always keep in mind the exact sound desired from the choir. Without an aural goal, there is little chance that the choir will develop into a group capable of communication. Then start looking for the good. All sounds that lead to or could lead to the conductor's aural goal are to be encouraged. What tone do you want from the women? Do they soar or screech? How do men handle the upper voice? Can they use falsetto? Exactly what sound do you want to hear on each vowel that the choir produces? Can you demonstrate it? Showing what you want to hear rather than talking about it saves much time. Use a tape recorder to be certain that what you are demonstrating exactly corresponds to what you *think* you are demonstrating. Be aware that changes in seating patterns may have a profound effect on the sound of the choir. Instill in the singers a willingness to experiment.

Imagine, for instance, that the women are not producing the *exact* sound you want to hear. Begin by choosing two or three excellent singers and ask them to demonstrate the sound you want. Perhaps you will not succeed on the first attempt. Change the seating and try again. If this doesn't work, change one of the singers and experiment again with the seating arrangement. Keep trying till you have a trio that can produce a model sound. Work at this in a good-natured way without registering shock or horror at sounds you don't prefer. Say "good" or "good sound" when you hear what you want.

Once you have established a viable sound, ask everyone to listen to it. Then ask the other singers not to imitate the sound but to use their own voices in such a way that they become part of it. Perhaps the quality of the overall sound may somewhat change as you add voices, but it remains *una voce.* If the singers have difficulty producing a good sound on a particular text, try an "oo" vowel or a unison hum.

Gradually begin to apply this acceptable sound to the whole repertory. Be patient. Remember, this will take time. The secret, however, is never to give up. Always continue to work toward the sound you want.

Another suggestion. After you have explained something to the choir, stay with it till it is done correctly. Many conductors give all the correct instructions, only to move right on whether or not the choir has succeeded in producing the desired effect.

Your knowledge of choral development must translate into concrete results.

One very important rehearsal technique is to pay particular attention to the text of the selection. What does the text mean? What function does it play in the context within which the composition will be used? If the liturgical function of choral music is carefully thought out by the conductor and particular choral pieces are part of a well-coordinated liturgical plan, then share this information with the choir. It will help them understand why you have selected this music. The text will be more meaningful and will be communicated in a more meaningful way.

Whenever possible, use imagery and poetry to encourage the quality of sound you hope to obtain. Don't be afraid to employ "psychology." These techniques will help the choir sing in a way that the meaning of text and music is effectively communicated.

If you have an opportunity to observe a skilled choral director at work, take advantage of it. This can be very helpful in learning rehearsal techniques. Courses and workshops in choral development or methods will also help develop your own leadership abilities.

7

Tone and Good Singing:

The Principles

Good tone, like virtue, is something everyone wants to have, yet no one is quite sure how to obtain it. But perhaps good tone is not as elusive as it might seem. Although a definition may be hard to come by, most people recognize good tone when they hear it. Several factors are involved in its production.

First, an exact image of the sound that is desired must exist in the "mind's ear" of the conductor. This image offers a goal toward which specific objectives in each rehearsal can then move. When conductors have such a goal, they can encourage singing that is consistent with it. On the other hand, they can discourage all sounds that do not lead toward this goal. It is from experience, from hearing good choirs, from listening to recordings of excellent choral groups, that the conductor's tone-goal image is acquired.

Second, each singer should form an image of what a good tone is and how it feels. Listening to tapes of their singing will quickly allow the choir members to discover whether their composite sound corresponds to what they think it is. Taking time in a rehearsal to help individual voices will allow the members to hear and compare various kinds of tone. Furthermore, the choir may want to listen to examples of the desired tone from recordings, tapes, and the like. Simply making each member *aware* that there *is* a tone-goal and that each singer is accountable to the conductor in the process of moving toward that goal is a major step toward attaining good tone.

Third, since good tone is a result of good singing, the tone goal must be compatible with the principles of good singing which is the result of:

1. a consistently pleasant tone;

2. an ability to sustain this tone with perfect intonation;

3. a way of singing that will not exhaust the singer.

Singing in this fashion is not natural. The instinctive thing to do is to tighten the throat for higher tones, to drop the support at the end of phrases, and to gasp for breath. The principles of good singing, that is, the physical factors of singing, must be taught to the choir during rehearsals. If a director regularly works toward a mental, physical, and aural concept of good tone, then the result will be a sound that is beautiful, communicative, and perfectly suited to the choir.

The pyramid on page 41 illustrates the physical factors of good singing.

The elements presented within the pyramid indicate that each step in the process of singing depends on those below it. If posture is poor, the other factors will not be correct. If breathing is faulty, then nothing above it in the pyramid can be correct. To concentrate on diction without giving adequate attention to all the other physical factors of singing is wasted time.

In the private studio these factors are dealt with on an individual basis. But in a choir rehearsal we are dealing with many people at once. Here are some exercises and vocalization patterns that are intended for group use.

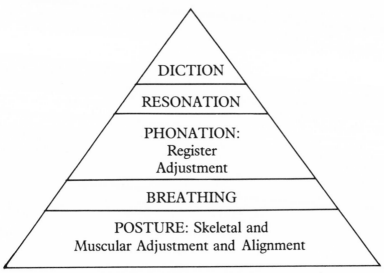

By permission: Burton A. Garlinghouse.

Posture. Have the choir members stand straight with the feet comfortably apart, one foot slightly in front of the other.

1. Pull the shoulders forward, up high, then back. On a signal from the director, release them. This gives the feeling of relaxation and exhilaration that occurs when unnecessary muscles are not involved in the area of the neck and shoulders. It gives the shoulders, back, and chest a high position without tension.

2. Ask the singers to imagine they are marionettes on a wire—a wire coming right out the top of the head. Ask them to swing the arms and torso about, imagining that just one wire is holding up the body.

Breathing. (First check posture.) Encourage diaphragmatic (abdominal area) breathing. Discourage clavicular (into the chest) breathing.

1. Laugh (belly laugh) with your singers. This shows where the

41

breathing and the source of muscular tension occur. A separate stroke of the diaphragm is used for each "hah."

2. Try panting exercises, but be careful not to hyperventilate.

3. Check the shoulder position of the singers as they take in air. Shoulders should remain in their original relaxed position and not be raised or "shrugged" as air is drawn into the body.

4. Have the singers exhale slowly using a hissing sound, controling and supporting the flow of air until the lungs are empty. The image of gently lifting the air up and out as the diaphragm slowly contracts is helpful in this exercise.

Phonation. (First check posture and breathing.) Proper phonation, so essential to good sound, is having throat space (an open throat) on all vowels and in all registers. Built on proper posture and breathing (support), it is coupled with loose jaw, tongue, and lips. The following exercises are designed to encourage proper phonation. The director should continuously listen for a sound that is free of tension.

Exercise 1:

yah yah yah yah   yah

Proceed with descending half steps. Keep jaw, lips, and tongue loose. Do not raise the jaw on the last note.

Exercise 2:

mong ming   mong ming   mong

ma   mo   ma   mo   ma *(f)*
mo   ma   mo   ma   mo *(m)*

In all two-phrase vocalises the inhalation between phrases must be inaudible and must not disturb the open, free throat position. The second inhalation should be timed to precede immediately the first note of the following phrase; it should not immediately follow the release of the last note of the first phrase.

Exercise 3:

hung- a - o - a - o - a - o - a
(also: a-i, a-e)

In vocalises employing the syllables "hung" (pronounced as in German) and "mong ming" make the vowel very short and sustain the "ng" hum with the jaw loose. The second half of the exercise feels the same as the first.

Exercise 4:

(m) iu   o   a   iu   o   a
(f) ha   o   a   ha   o   a

iu = "you"

Register adjustment is subconscious; it is easier to achieve and to sense register adjustment on descending vocalise patterns and in ascending and descending patterns involving larger intervals. Avoid ascending diatonic scale patterns in group vocalizing.

Basses, baritones, and tenors should be encouraged to slip into falsetto or a very light head voice for high notes which involve any strain.

Resonation. (First check posture, breathing, and phonation.)Resonation or "ring" in the sound is likely to occur when phonation is correct. The singer senses a vibration in the middle of the face—teeth, nose. To encourage awareness of this sensation as part of good singing, also try humming (with teeth slightly apart and plenty of space in the mouth) and exercise with consonants (Z, V, M, N) that cause this sensation. Listen for the ring in the sound. Its presence means that the singer is on the right track.

Diction. (First check posture, breathing, phonation, and resonation.) If the choir has good diction, the listener will be able to understand the words. Confer the bibliography for specific books on diction. Supple lips and tongue will permit the necessary formation of correct vowel and consonant sounds. All the tension comes from down below (the belly); keep the lips, jaw, and tongue loose. Good diction, then, is possible only when the other physical factors of singing are correct.

A choir's tone is its principal product. Control of choral tone is achieved only when the choir itself has come to know its own sound. For this to happen, each singer must become personally involved in the process of control.

8

So You Want to Hire

a Choir Director

When a parish decides to hire a choir director, the first temptation is to telephone someone who can help find the best musician available. Unfortunately, this nebulous "best musician" may not turn out to be the best person for the position the parish has in mind, if indeed there is anything in mind other than a vague notion that a choir director somehow or other gets the choir to sing at Mass on Sunday. Although there is nothing wrong with seeking outside help, certain steps should be taken before this happens. In this way a parish can properly formulate its needs and expectations: first, for its own benefit; second, for the benefit of those who assist in the search process; third, for the benefit of the musician who will be hired.

The following are some questions that might help the parish as it begins to search for a director.

1. How do we envision the role of music in our parish's liturgical celebrations? (The *General Instruction of the Roman Missal* and the bishops' document *Music in Catholic Worship* will be especially helpful in answering this question.)

2. How important is worship to our community? How important is music in liturgy?

3. What are our dreams, expectations, and goals?

4. How well have we realized out goals in regard to liturgical music?

5. How should parish musicians interact with one another and with the overall parish structure? How is liturgy planned in the parish? How well does the planning procedure work?

6. What musical skills do we expect from a musician? What level of expertise are we looking for?

When these questions have been answered, or at least discussed, it is possible to draft a job description, so that everyone applying for the opening will know just what will be expected. The parish says "this is what we want you to do."

Be specific in drafting the job description. Try to explain what you expect the musician to do, not only in the regular worship life of the parish but also in terms of special liturgies, meetings, and the like. A few calls to established choir directors in the area can be very useful in determining the scope of the job you are offering.

Also be specific about salary. Phrases like "salary negotiable" or "salary calculated according to experience and training" are simply time wasters. However, it is useful to give a salary range (for example, "salary from $15,000 to $20,000, depending on . . . "); at least applicants will then know whether to apply. If not much money is available, say so, but be sure to mention other attractive aspects of the parish (for example, "salary $3,000 now, but equitable salary as parish continues to grow"). Additional factors for the organist/director would be teaching privileges and a clear understanding as to wedding and funeral income. For a full-time position also describe such benefits as health insurance, pension plans, and the like.

A question that often surfaces at this stage is whether the parish should employ a choir director or a combined organist/

director. Most would agree that the ideal situation would be to have a superb director working with a talented and cooperative organist/pianist. But sometimes only a limited amount of money is available. When this is divided between two salaries, the amount for each salary is too low to attract the best persons. One solution is to pay one person to assume both roles, conductor and organist, so that an attractive salary is available. Some parishes have written several job descriptions in order not to exclude talented musicians. But remember that conducting from the console is a specialized and demanding skill: not everyone who plays well and conducts well can do both at the same time. There just aren't too many of these persons available.

Many dioceses now publish guidelines to help parishes formulate job descriptions and salary standards for their musicians. Contact your Diocesan Worship Commission. Also, the FDLC (Federation of Diocesan Liturgical Commissions, P.O. Box 29039, Washington, D.C. 20017) publishes a *Survey Report on Guidelines for Just Compensation of Liturgical Musicians* which lists and describes many of the guidelines issued by dioceses in this country.

The AGO (American Guild of Organists) offers several guides on financial compensation. One is *Music in the Church: Work and Compensation* (Seattle Chapter). Another is *The Work and Compensation of the Church Musician* (Boston Chapter). Also consult with local churches that have excellent liturgical music programs.

Although each parish will formulate a job description reflecting its own needs, the following two samples are representative, one for an organist/director, the other for a minister of music.

*   *   *

Announcement of Anticipated Position Vacancy

Director of Music

Organist and Choirmaster

Qualifications. Competence in organ performance; competence in conducting and choral development; working knowledge of Roman Catholic liturgy; organizational and administrative skills; interpersonal skills in working with a professional and volunteer music program.

Duties. Three weekend Eucharists (Saturday, 5:00 PM; Sunday, 10:00 AM; 12:00 PM; additional liturgies on Christmas, during Holy Week, and on Easter; music for weddings, funerals, confirmation, special celebrations; a choral rehearsal (traditionally Thursday evening) and Sunday morning rehearsal before the Mass.

The Program. The Sunday 10:00 Eucharist involves the choir/cantors/soloists; the other two celebrations employ cantor/organ and congregational song. The professional staff numbers six singers (SATTBB). The volunteer choir has approximately twenty-five members.

The Instrument. In late January 1987 a new 26 rank mechanical instrument constructed by the Schudi Organ Company will be installed in a fine and reverberant structure; the instrument will repose in the rear gallery.

Remuneration. The salary is considered approximately half-time in the range of $10,000 to $15,000. Additional compensation is derived through weddings and funerals.

To Apply. Send a complete resume, detailing educational background and all appropriate professional experience. Write a short letter describing your understanding of music in the Roman Catholic Church today. Forward this information to: ____.

*   *   *

Minister of Music - Job Description

The Minister of Music, a member of the Pastoral Staff, is responsible for the planning, preparation, and performance of all music in the parish. This person shall be available for regular consultation with the Pastor and shall be an ex-officio member of all parish worship, liturgy, or music committees.

1. The Music Minister is responsible for the procurement, inventory, maintenance, use, and disposal of the music library and all musical equipment. He or she is also responsible for the auditioning, acceptance, hiring, and termination of all persons performing or teaching music in the parish, whether paid musicians or volunteers. The Music Minister assists in the hiring and supervising of a folk choir director, school music teacher, and children's choir director. He or she is also responsible for supplying soloists or instrumentalists as needed.

2. The Music Minister is responsible for organ and/or instrumental music at the Saturday evening and Sunday morning Masses, for a cantor to lead singing at Sunday Masses, and for regular rehearsals of the various choirs. It is understood that the regular choir season is from the Sunday following Labor Day through the feast of Corpus Christi. Additional Masses requiring music include those on Holy Days of Obligation, Thanksgiving, Ash Wednesday, Holy Thursday, Good Friday, and the Easter Vigil. This may involve delegation to a folk group rather than organ and cantor or choir.

3. Weddings, funerals, and other services requiring music are the responsibility of the Minister, who shall work with the parties involved to plan music appropriate to the occasion. The Minister is the designated organist for such occasions unless he or she chooses to retain another, or if other *parish* musicians are used in lieu of organ. The Minister is responsible for the musical quality and content in all parish celebrations. The prearranged standard fee includes performance at the service from the organist's standard repertoire plus consultation with the parties

involved. Special music, rehearsals, and the like will incur additional fees determined by the Minister, based on particular circumstances.

4. The Minister of Music shall be available to teachers or groups within the parish (including the school) to provide direction and encouragement in the study and performance of music. The Minister is responsible for the hiring and training of the parish cantors, including the selection of the cantors' repertoire. The Minister will also oversee any necessary revisions in the parish "folk hymnal" as the need arises.

5. The Minister of Music shall prepare an annual budget (1 July through 30 June) for the music department. This budget shall be submitted for the approval of the Pastor and/or the Finance Committee.

6. Paid vacation and/or study leave consists of four weeks, for which the services of a substitute organist (only) may be required if requested by the Pastor. Sick leave is subject to the discretion of the Pastor.

7. The parish will provide the Minister with suitable office and work space including desk, telephone, and file cabinets and shelving space as necessary. It will also provide adequate choir rehearsal facilities at a regular time and place each week.

8. The Minister of Music is directly responsible to the Pastor, and any direction or guidance in the performance of the Minister's duties will come through the Pastor. The contract for employment is an annual one, normally from 1 July through 30 June, whether written or oral. The music budget, including the Minister's salary, is subject to annual review. There is to be at least a minimum yearly increase to reflect the "cost of living." Termination of this agreement by either party is subject to a minimum of 30 days notice, normally at the end of the contract period.

Bibliography

Decker, Harold A. and Julius Herford, eds. *Choral Conducting: A Symposium.* New York: Appleton-Century-Crofts, 1973.

Ehmann, Wilhelm. *Choral Directing.* Minneapolis: Augsburg Publishing House, 1968.

Finn, W. J. *The Art of the Choral Conductor.* Evanston: Summy-Birchard Co., 1960.

Garretson, Robert L. *Conducting Choral Music.* Boston: Allyn and Bacon, Inc., 1980.

Howerton, George. *Technique and Style in Choral Conducting.* New York: Carl Fischer Inc., 1957.

Lamb, Gordon. *Choral Techniques.* Second edition. Dubuque: Wm. C. Brown Co., 1979.

Marshall, Madeleine. *The Singer's Manual of English Diction.* New York: G. Schirmer, Inc., 1953.

McElheran, Brock. *Conducting Techniques.* New York: Oxford University Press, 1966.

Moe, Daniel. *Basic Choral Concepts.* Minneapolis: Augsburg Publishing House, 1972.

Robinson, Ray and Allen Winold. *The Choral Experience.* New York: Harper's College Press, 1976.

Vennard, Wm. *Singing, the Mechanism and the Technique.* Revised edition. New York: Carl Fischer, 1967.

Wilson, Harry. *Artistic Choral Singing.* New York: G. Schirmer, Inc., 1959.

Repertoire

Renaissance

Aichinger, Gregor	Regina coeli (Arista)	E-M Easter
Byrd, William	Ave verum corpus (Oxford)	M
Byrd, William	Ego sum panis (Broude)	M
Croce, Giovanni	O sacrum convivium (Arista)	M

Farrant, Richard	Two English Anthems
	   Hide Not Thou Thy
	     Face
	   Call to Remembrance
	(Hinshaw)
		M-D

Gibbons, Orlando	Almighty and Everlasting God (Oxford)	E-M
Gibbons, Orlando	O Lord Increase My Faith (Novello)	M
Guerrero, Francisco	Canite tuba (Concordia)	M Advent

Hassler, Hans Leo	Cantate Domino (E.C. Schirmer)	M
Isaac, Heinrich	O esca viatorum (GIA)	E
Lassus, Orlando	Jubilate Deo (Arista)	M
Marenzio, Claudio	Hodie Christus natus est (Concordia)	M Christmas
Palestrina, G.P.	Ego sum panis (Arista)	D
Palestrina, G.P.	O bone Jesu (Schott)	E
Palestrina, G.P.	O sacrum convivium (Breitkopf)	M
Palestrina, G.P.	Panis angelicus (GIA)	M
Palestrina, G.P.	Sicut cervus desiderat (Arista)	M
Pitoni, Giuseppe	Cantate Domino (Bourne)	M
Sweelinck, J.P.	Hode Christus natus est (Novello)	D SSATB Christmas
Tallis, Thomas	If Ye Love Me (H.W. Gray)	M
Tallis, Thomas	That Virgin's Child (Frank Music Corp.)	E

Victoria, Tomas Luis	Jesu dulcis memoria (Broude)	M
Victoria, Tomas Luis	O magnum mysterium (Arista)	M-D

Baroque

Bach, J.S.	Alleluia [BWV 230] (Broude)	D
Bach, J.S.	Alleluia, O Praise the Lord Most Holy (Concordia)	M
Bach, J.S.	Awake, Thou Wintry Earth (E.C. Schirmer)	E Easter
Bach, J.S.	Break Forth, O Beauteous Heavenly Light [Christmas Oratorio] (G. Schirmer)	E
Bach, J.S.	Jesu, Joy of Man's Desiring (E.C. Schirmer)	E
Boyce, William Richard Proulx (arr.)	Alleluia Round (GIA)	E
Buxtehude, Dietrich	In te Domine speravi (Arista)	M

Handel, G.F.	And the Glory of the Lord [Messiah] (G. Schirmer)	M-D
Handel, G.F.	For unto Us [Messiah] (G. Schirmer)	M-D
Handel, G.F.	Hallelujah [Messiah] (G. Schirmer)	M-D
Handel, G.F.	Jesus, Sun of Life, My Splendor (Concordia)	E
Handel, G.F.	Praise the Lord [Judas Maccabeus] (Flammer)	E
Jungst	Christmas Hymn (G. Schirmer)	E Christmas
Praetorius, Michael	Lo, How a Rose E'er Blooming [Christmas Oratorio] (G. Schirmer)	E
Purcell, Henry	O Be Joyful in the Lord (Word)	M
Purcell, Henry	Rejoice in the Lord Always (Concordia)	M
Purcell, Henry	Thou Knowest, Lord, the Secrets of Our Hearts (Novello)	M

Classical

Cherubini, Luigi A. Lovelace (arr.)	Like As a Father (Choristers Guild)	E
Cherubini, Luigi W. Riegger (arr.)	Veni Jesu (Flammer)	E
Gasparini, Francesco (attr. Mozart)	Adoramus te (Arista)	M
Haydn, Joseph	In Thee, O Lord (Fox)	E
Haydn, Joseph	The Heavens Are Telling [Creation] (G. Schirmer)	M
Haydn, Michael	Timete Dominum (G. Schirmer)	M
Mozart, Wolfgang	Ave verum (Arista)	M
Mozart, Wolfgang	Laudate Dominum (E.C. Schirmer)	M
Mozart, Wolfgang	Regina coeli (Breitkopf)	M Easter

Romantic

Attwood, Thomas	Teach Me, O Lord (Harris)	M

Berlioz, Hector	The Shepherd's Farewell to the Holy Family [Childhood of Christ] (E.C. Schirmer)	M Christmas
Brahms, Johannes	How Lovely Is Thy Dwelling Place [Ein Deutsches Requiem] (E.C. Schirmer)	D
Brahms, Johannes	Let Nothing Ever Grieve Thee (Peters)	M
Elgar, Edward	Ave verum (Novello)	M
Franck, Cesar	Psalm 150 (J. Fischer)	M
Goss, John	O Savior of the World (G. Schirmer)	M
Ireland, John	Greater Love Hath No Man (Galaxy)	M-D
Mendelssohn, F.	Cast Thy Burden [Elijah] (G. Schirmer)	E
Mendelssohn, F.	He That Shall Endure [Elijah] (G. Schirmer)	M
Mendelssohn, F.	He Watching over Israel	D

58

	[Elijah] (G. Schirmer)	
Mendelssohn, F.	How Lovely Are the Messengers [St. Paul] (G. Schirmer)	M
Mendelssohn, F.	Lift Thine Eyes [Elijah] (G. Schirmer)	M SSA
Mendelssohn, F.	See What Love Hath the Father [St. Paul] (Augsburg)	M
Mendelssohn, F.	There Shall a Star (Kjos)	M
Saint-Saens, Camille	Tollite hostias (Carl Fischer)	E
Stainer, John	God So Loved the World [Crucifixion] (G. Schirmer)	M
Tschesnokoff, P.G.	Let Thy Holy Presence (Pro Art)	M
Wesley, Samuel	Lead Me, Lord (E.C. Schirmer)	E

Contemporary

Aston, Peter	O Sing unto the Lord (RSCM)	M

Beebe, Hank	The Lord Is My Light (Hinshaw)	M-D
Berger, Jean	The Eyes of All Wait upon Thee (Augsburg)	M
Carter, John	How Beautiful upon the Mountains (Hinshaw)	M
Chepponis, James	Lenten Proclamation (GIA)	E Lent
Christiansen, Paul (arr.)	Wondrous Love (Augsburg)	M Lent
Dawson, William (arr.)	Ain'a That Good News (Kjos)	M-D
Dawson, William (arr.)	Mary Had a Baby (Kjos)	M Christmas
Dawson, William (arr.)	There Is a Balm (Kjos)	E-M
Distler, Hugo	Lo! How a Rose E'er Blooming (Concordia)	M Christmas
Durufle, Marcel	Ubi caritas [from Quatre Motets] (Durand)	D

Englert, Eugene	Sing to Him of Praise Eternal (GIA)	M
Fleming, L.L.	Three about Jesus Every Time I Think about Jesus Give Me Jesus Ride On, King Jesus (Augsburg)	M-D
Friedell, Harold	Draw Us in the Spirit's Tether (H.W. Gray)	M
Harris, William H.	Behold, the Tabernacle of God (RSCM)	M
Holst, Gustav	Let All Mortal Flesh Keep Silence (Galaxy)	E
Holst, Gustav	Lullay My Liking (G. Schirmer)	M Christmas
Hopson, Hal (arr.)	The Gift of Love (Hope Publishing Co.)	E 2 part
Hovland, Egil	The Glory of the Father (Walton)	M
Hunter, Robert (arr.)	Oh, Kind Jesus (Carl Fischer)	E
Hurd, David	Teach Me O Lord (GIA)	E

Ives, Charles	A Christmas Carol (Merion Music)	M Christmas
Joncas, Michael	Every Stone Shall Cry (Cooperative Music; avail- able from Oregon Catholic Press)	M
Joubert, John	There Is No Rose (Novello)	M-D Christmas
Kreutz, Robert	Gift of Finest Wheat (Board of Governors, Forty-First International Eucharistic Congress, Inc.)	M
Leaf, Robert	God's Spirit As a Wind Doth Move (GIA)	M-D
Leaf, Robert	That Easter Morn at Break of Day (Augsburg)	E Easter
Manz, Paul	E'en So Lord Jesus, Quickly Come (Concordia)	M
Marshall, Jane	Awake, My Heart (H.W. Gray)	M
Marshall, Jane	Eternal Light (GIA)	E
Marshall, Jane	Happy Are You In Thee O Lord (Augsburg)	E E

Martin, G.	Lord Jesus Chrst, We Humbly Pray (H.W. Gray)	E
Moe, Daniel	Fanfare and Choral Procession (Augsburg)	M Easter
Nicolson, Sidney Schalk, C. (arr.)	Lift High the Cross (Concordia)	M Easter
Owens, Sam Batt	Take My Life and Let It Be (Choristers Guild)	E 2 part
Parker, Alice (arr.) Shaw, Robert (arr.)	I Will Arise (Lawson Gould)	E-M
Peeters, Flor	Entrada festiva (Peters)	E Easter or Festival
Pelz, Walter	Show Me Thy Ways (Augsburg)	M
Petrich, Roger	Choral Variations on "Ah, Holy Jesus" (Oxford)	M
Pfautsch, Lloyd	Fanfare for Easter (Flammer)	M Easter
Pfautsch, Lloyd	His Spirit Leads On (Lawson)	D Easter
Powell, Robert	Anima Christi (Augsburg)	E

Proulx, Richard (arr.)	Amazing Grace (GIA)	E	
Proulx, Richard	Behold, Now the House of God (Augsburg)	M	
Proulx, Richard	Christmas Processional (GIA)	E	Christmas
Proulx, Richard	Praise the Savior Now and Ever (Schmitt, Hall and McCreary)	E	
Proulx, Richard	Psalm 134 (GIA)	E-M	
Proulx, Richard	This Is the Day (GIA)	E	Easter
Rorem, Ned	Three Hymn Anthems Peters	M	
Rutter, John	Christ the Lord Is Risen Again (Oxford)	M	Easter
Rutter, John	I Will Lift Up Mine Eyes (Oxford)	M-D	
Rutter, John	O Clap Your Hands (Oxford)	D	
Schalk, Carl	Now (Agape - Hope)	M	

Shaw, Martin	With a Voice of Singing (G. Schirmer)	M
Somary, Johannes	Jesus My Lord, My God, My All (GIA)	E
Thompson, Randall	Alleluia (E.C. Schirmer)	D
Titcomb, Everett	I Will Not Leave You Comfortless (Carl Fischer)	M
Toolan, Suzanne	The Call (GIA)	E
Vaughan Williams, R.	O How Amiable (Oxford)	E
Vaughan Williams, R.	O Taste and See (Oxford)	M
Vaughan Williams, R.	The Old Hundreth Psalm Tune (Oxford)	E
Vermulst, Jan	Where Charity and Love Prevail (World Library Publications)	M
Weaver, John	Epiphany Alleluias (Boosey and Hawkes)	M-D

Weber, Paul D.	Psalm 32 (Augsburg)	E-M SAB
Westendorf, Omer	Stewards of the Earth [Sibelius, Finlandia] (World Library Publications)	E
White, E.J.	A Prayer of St. Richard (Oxford)	E
Wood, Dale	Christ Is Made the Sure Foundation (Schmitt, Hall and McCreary)	E
Wood, Dale	Jubilate Deo (Augsburg)	E
Young, Carlton	Hearts and Voices Raise [O filii et filiae] (Augsburg)	E
Zgodava, Richard (arr.)	Noel Nouvelet (Augsburg)	M Christmas

Service Music: English Mass Settings

Alstott, Owen	Good Shepherd Mass (Oregon Catholic Press)	E
Alstott, Owen	Heritage Mass (Oregon Catholic Press)	E
Aston, Peter	Holy Communion, Series 3 (RSCM)	E

Daly, Margaret	St. Benedict Centenary Mass (Irish Institute of Pastoral Liturgy)	E
Foley, John	Glory to God (NALR)	E
Haugen, Marty	Mass of Creation (GIA) The complete eucharistic prayer is set to music— presider's part available	M
Hillert, Richard	Glory to God [Festival Liturgy] (GIA)	E
Hopson, Hal	Mass for the People (GIA)	M
Hughes, Howard	Mass of the Divine Word (GIA)	M
Hughes, Howard	Misa de San Jose (GIA)	M
Hurd, David	New Plainsong Mass (GIA)	E
Isele, David Clark	Lamb of God [from the Holy Cross Mass] (GIA)	E
Isele, David Clark	Notre Dame Mass (GIA)	E

Kreutz, Robert	Mass for an American Saint (World Library Publications)	M
Mathias, William	Communion Service, Series 3 (Oxford)	M
Near, Gerald	Communion Service (H.W. Gray)	M-D
Peloquin, Alex	Glory to God [Mass of the Bells] (GIA)	E
Proulx, Richard	A Community Mass (GIA)	E
Proulx, Richard	A Festival Eucharist (GIA)	E-M
Proulx, Richard	Mass of the Redeemer (GIA)	M
Rutter, John	Communion Service, Series 3 (Oxford)	E
Schiavone, John	Mass in Honor of All Saints (GIA)	M
Walker, Christopher	Sanctus in "Nativitate" (Oregon Catholic Press)	M
Williamson, Malcom	Agnus Dei (Boosey and Hawkes)	M

Williamson, Malcom	Agnus Dei (Boosey and Hawkes)	M

Service Music: Latin Mass Settings

Dufay, Guillaume	Gloria ad modum tubae (GIA)	M
Hassler, Hans Leo	Missa secunda (Fischer)	M
Monteverdi, Claudio	Gloria from Messa a quattro voci (GIA)	M
Palestrina, G.P.	Missa aeterna Christi munera (Arista)	D
Viadana, Ludovico	Missa "L'hora passa" (Arista)	M

Service Music: Psalm Settings

Alstott, Owen	Respond and Acclaim (Oregon Catholic Press)	
Gelineau, Joseph	The Gelineau Gradual (GIA)	
Isele, David Clark	Psalms for the Church Year (GIA)	
Marty Haugen/ David Haas	Psalms for the Church Year (GIA)	

Kreutz, Robert   Psalms
                  (Oregon Catholic Press)

Addresses of Publishers

Arista Music Company
PO Box 1596
Brooklyn NY 11201

Augsburg Publishing
426 S. Fifth Street
Minneapolis MN 55440

Boosey & Hawkes
200 Smith Street
Farmingdale NY 11752

Bourne Co.
437 Fifth Avenue
New York NY 10016

Breitkopf and Haertel
[Alexander Broude, Inc.]
225 W. 57th Street
New York NY 10019

Alexander Broude, Inc.
225 W. 57th Street
New York NY 10019

Choristers Guild
PO Box 38118
Dallas TX 75238

Concordia Publishing House
3558 S. Jefferson Avenue
St. Louis MO 63118

Durand
[Theodore Presser Co.]
Presser Place
Bryn Mawr PA 19096

Carl Fischer Inc.
56-62 Cooper Square
New York NY 10003

J. Fischer & Bro.
Belwin-Mills Publishing Corp.
1776 Broadway
New York NY 10019

Harold Flammer
[Shawnee Press]
Del Water Gap PA 18327

Sam Fox Music Co.
170 N.E. 33rd Street
Ft. Lauderdale FL 33334

Frank Music Corp.
[Hal Leonard Publishing Co.]
8112 W. Bluemound Road
Milwaukee WI 532113

Galaxy Music
[E.C. Schirmer]
2121 Broadway
New York NY 10023

70

GIA Publications
7404 S. Mason Avenue
Chicago IL 60638

H.W. Gray Publications
[Belwin-Mills Publishing Corp.]
1776 Broadway
New York NY 10019

Harris Music Publications
PO Box 1356
Ft. Worth TX 76101

Hinshaw Music Inc.
Box 470
Chapel Hill NC 27514

Hope Publishing Co.
380 South Main Street
Carol Stream IL 60187

Irish Institute of Pastoral Liturgy
College Street
Carlow, Ireland

Kjos Music Company
4382 Jutland Drive
San Diego CA 92117

Lawson Gould Publishing
[G. Schirmer]
866 Third Avenue
New York NY 10022

Merion Music
[Theodore Presser]
Presser Place
Bryn Mawr PA 19096

North American Liturgy Resources
10802 North 23rd Avenue
Phoenix AZ 85029

Novello Publications
[Theodore Presser]
Presser Place
Bryn Mawr PA 19096

Oregon Catholic Press
5536 NE Hassalo
Portland OR 97213

Oxford University Press
200 Madison Avenue
New York NY 10016

C.F. Peters Corp.
373 Park Avenue South
New York NY 10016

Pro Art Publications Inc.
Box 234
Westbury NY 11590

RSCM
Royal School of Church Music
Addington Palace
Croyden, Surrey
England

E.C. Schirmer Music Company
112 South Street
Boston MA 02111

G. Schirmer, Inc.
866 Third Avenue
New York NY 10022

Schmitt, Hall and McCreary
88 South 10th Street
Minneapolis MN 55403

Schott
European American Music
195 Allwood Road
Clifton NJ 07012

Walton Music Corp.
170 NE 33rd Street
Ft. Lauderdale FL 33334

Word Inc.
PO Box 1790
Waco TX 76703

World Library Publications
3759 Willow Road
Schiller Park IL 60176